Know My Voice II

GOD HAS A KINGDOM, AND IT IS NOT ORGANIZED RELIGION!

by

Rev. Dr. John Diomede

To order additional copies of this book, contact:
Proisle publishing Services LLC
1177 6th Ave 5th Floor
New York, NY 10036, USA
Phone: (+1 347-922-3779)
info@proislepublishing.com

PROISLE PUBLISHING

My Sheep Know My Voice

My sheep listen to my voice; I know them, and they follow me. [28] I give them eternal life, and they shall never perish; no one will snatch them out of my hand. (Joh 10:27-28 NIV)

Dedicated

To my Parents
Rachel and Edward

To My Mentors

Marvin

John

Bill

Dan

The Holy Spirit provided me with them.
They gave to me
wisdom, love, discipline and guidance
in a timely manner
for His Kingdom.

Table of Contents

Introduction

The Bible is a book that draws out a host of emotions in people. Some people love the idea of it, keep it by the side of their bed and try to live by its commands by being a good person in their everyday life. Then there are people who consider the book as completely irrelevant. There are those who only encounter it occasionally and not for any significant purpose. Lastly, there are those who despise it. As time has gone on it occurs to me that the Bible is less and less used in the secular community, a situation that I hope changes on an individual basis. One reason, as described by one of my sons, is its density, where the subject matter is concerned. I get it and I know why. It is my desire to give relevance to the book in a way that is not common and to make it part of everyday thinking. I also have seen the bible being used incorrectly in the religious community. Many in the religious community use specific verses as a manipulative tool to undergird and protect their established conclusions. The Bible is not a religious book, it is a book that details relational interaction. The relational interaction in these texts is far more robust than any modern-day mystery writer and has life altering potential[1]. For the reader to develop a sense of relational thinking, we must stop looking at the text in its entirety and look at the encounters recorded therein, especially where they share commonality with the readers life. Much of what I speak about, relationship with God, and many of the foundational thoughts[2] expressed biblically about that relationship are shared by many people under the umbrella of the relational concepts and dictates found in these texts, including Jew, Christian and Muslim. As one indulges this thought process, they will realize a host of connections that will draw them to The Holy Spirit of God, the source of relationship.

This is a test of the emergency broadcast system

Consider the following list of comments
- Abortion should be banned completely

---

[1] "You don't just read the Bible, you must inquire of it."[1]
Metaxas, Eric. Bonhoeffer: Pastor, Martyr, Prophet, Spy. Nashville: Thomas Nelson Publishing, 2010.

[2] He has shown you, O mortal, what is good. And what does the LORD require of you? To act justly and to love mercy and to walk humbly with your God. Micah 6:8

- A woman's right to choose should be preserved up to the point of delivery
- The 2020 election was stolen from Donald Trump
- Obama was not born a US citizen
- The Obama birther issue is a complete falsehood
- Global warming is a myth
- Republicans are ignorant for following Trump
- Climate change should be Funded by the government as a significant issue of our time
- Institutional racism exists throughout all areas of government
- Black Lives Matter movement is a racist movement
- Black Lives Matter movement is needed to protect Blacks
- Martin Luther King was a racist
- Martin Luther King was a great man
- Christianity is inherently racist
- Guns should be legal to carry in any state
- Guns should be banned

- Women should not be allowed to be broadcasters for men's sports
- Social media should not be controlled in any way
- Freedom of speech is dangerous
- Gays should not be allowed to serve in the military
- Gays should not be discriminated against in any way
- The news tells the truth all the time
- The news is fake

This list of comments is meant to give you an opportunity to think about any one of those issues and draw some thoughts to the surface, a self-test. As you consider these thoughts consider the fact that some of those thoughts were not your own. The mind is the playing field for your life's events. Just like any other field, you are not the only one present at the game, an especially important concept to consider.

Something else to consider is that the world we live in is angry and it is becoming more and more angry every day. This is due to what happens in our minds.

We believe the anger is sourced by society's events, but it is not, the source is the mind. Additionally, I can't be sure if the world is as angry as it was five hundred or a thousand years ago, but I do know that the anger is much more widespread because communication is more widespread. To put it another way, a spark a thousand years ago could have started a forest fire. Today a spark can ignite a world of fire because the world has become an exceedingly small place.

Religion is the blinder pulled down over our eyes

Most people know the story of Adam and Eve and most of them have an opinion on the topic. But whether it is factual or not is irrelevant for this conversation. What is relevant is that there were multiple participants involved in the story. Here is a list of the participants:

1. Adam (represents an individual)
2. Eve (represents an individual)

3. Adam and Eve (represent the community/world)

4. The serpent (represents the demonic/enemy)

5. God (represents God)

As you thought through the first list of comments there were multiple voices working inside of you. The previous list encompasses all the voices that you hear inside of your mind. Let me break down the list even further to be more relevant.

1. Voice of self
    a. Your voice
2. Voice of the world
    a. Family and friends
    b. The Media
        i. TV, email, websites, cell phone, etc.
    c. The church
    d. work
    e. Politics
3. The voice of the Demonic realm
    a. Thoughts of Apathy, fear, Anger, frustration, untruths, want, sadness, revenge, depression, hate, violence etc.

4. The voice of God (the Holy Spirit)

   a. Thoughts of love, joy, peace, patience, gentleness, goodness, faithfulness, kindness, self-control, compassion, mercy, etc.

Religion is a system that attempts to tell us the right way to act in life. Its intention is to represent God or to be the voice of God. Some religious organizations use the Bible to support this concept and others have their own holy books. As an individual, one can choose to abide by or reject the organizational constructs. Whatever you conclude is based on the opinion from one or more of the four voices Over the years people have told me that they are much smarter than religious organizations. They know better. When a Christian, for example, tells someone that a mass murderer can make it to heaven just by asking Jesus to forgive him, usually the hearer realizes that there is a disconnect somewhere. Two voices can compete for compassion. One for the victim, another for the penitent offender. On the cross Jesus was flanked by two individuals who heard two of the voices. One heard rebuke, anger, and fear. The other was penitent because he heard the voice of God. So, what is one to do about this problem? How do we resolve the different thoughts/voices? Religion and religious leaders all have an opinion on this and many other topics, opinions that organizations claim God would agree with. But most of us know that there are often two or more sides to resolving religious and secular conundrums. What if we could go to the source? What would God say if you could actually speak to the Creator, maybe have lunch? Many of us would like to have that audience, like people do with the Pope or President. I am here to tell you that God wants to give you that audience. Religion prevents this meeting in too many cases[3]. And too many people refuse to stand up and ask, is it really possible for me to hear the voice of the Holy Spirit? They fear they will be mocked. Religion has concealed God for millennia. Individuals throughout history, such as Martin Luther, have attempted to challenge the process but, the human life is short. He challenged doctrinal mandates that God did not command. When the spark of a Martin Luther, a person who heard from God dies, the

---

[3] "But woe to you, scribes and Pharisees, hypocrites, because you shut off the kingdom of heaven from men; for you do not enter in yourselves, nor do you allow those who are entering to go in. (Mat 23:13 NAS)

movement usually takes on an organizational cloak and the voice of the Holy Spirit gets drowned out by the other voices, producing yet another religious organizational outcome. Every time this happened historically, the organization redevelops dogma which can block the individual from seeing the relationship that God desires.

Righteous Indignation

Indignation is anger directed at something perceived unfair. The Bible has many verses indicating God's and man's indignation. The indignation of the God of the Bible is varied, sometimes directed at His people and other times directed at the oppressors of His people. Man's indignation is also varied, sometimes asking God to repay the oppressors, and other times as an expression of the weariness produced by dealing with human brokenness. I believe it is fair to say that we all experience righteous indignation at times. The question of the validity of righteous indignation has less to do with the presence of the thought and has more to do with the accuracy of the feeling. For example, when we experience this anger, is the feeling valid? As you can imagine, perspective plays a huge role in this process. And because of this, we may have an opportunity begin to reevaluate how we have understood an idea, maybe for many years. Today, the world is redefining definitions that have existed for a long time. Redefinition can be a problem because relationships can become moving targets. Christianity is being redefined. If it is revealed that a person is a Christian and you happen to be white, in many cases it is assumed that they don't like or are uncomfortable around gays and are labeled prejudice. This is a huge error and a profound example of redefinition. Redefinition also can be used to manipulate relationships. We must reevaluate with the help of the Holy Spirit so we can determine how to live without the bias of definition or redefinition that is driven by the voice of the world or the voice of the demonic. As we reevaluate, we may have the opportunity to see through the eyes of The Holy Spirit and how God defines a matter. Let us examine the topic of homosexuality. When one is righteously indignant against the homosexual, that person allows the act to become more important than the person. Because of the <u>world's</u> voice of indignation, the more important information espoused by the Holy Spirit does not necessarily make it to the surface. That information is the fact that God, repeatedly, seeks followers that are compassionate, not judgmental. This is also true of the Quran[4]. Many verses in both books seek to bind humanity together and, the real indignation of God is usually referenced to individuals who do not love one another, who do not respect one another, and who are not compassionate toward each other. The voice of the Holy Spirit guides the mind away from anger and towards unity. God's anger will be made manifest at some point in time but unless you claim you are a prophet of God, judgement is not your responsibility. Let's you and I lay down our anger by hearing from the Holy Spirit, so God's anger is not directed at us later on. Let God be God, He is the judge.

---

[4] "God is not merciful to one who is not merciful". The Study Quran, note on 48:29 at 74.94

To redefine or not to redefine, that is the question!

My original list of comments can be considered either right or wrong, good or bad, common sense or non-sensical depending on your perspective and priorities. My perspective on many situations has changed over time. At some point in my life, I began to see human brokenness, mostly my own but then, as I considered others perspective, the brokenness became replete within all humanity. I realized that some of my conclusions about people and life did not consider the depth of the human soul and how different we all are inside. I have high school friends who have been on the other side of the aisle before I knew there was an aisle. Then, for a long time, I defended my side of the aisle. Who is right? Who is wrong? Is there a right or wrong or a good or bad when it comes to politics, religion, the human soul, or is it just perspective? I have since stopped defending my perspective because I became convinced that there was a perspective that overrides all human perspectives, God's perspective! What is your perspective on culture, politics, race, religion? Are you willing to challenge your perspective by reevaluating what you know by definition and allow the Holy Spirit to offer a new perspective? One of compassion. Additionally, one tool of the demonic voice is manipulation. It uses human language, redefined words, name calling, to brand the other side of the aisle as evil. If evaluated properly, one would see this is simply a cyclical process to keep human hating human. The demonic use race, ethnicity, religion, political opinion, immigration, and sexuality as buzz topics to keep the hate alive. Honestly, at this point I could care less about politics, religion, ideologies, and cultures. The way the media and the internet present these issues cannot be trusted because they have been changing the definitions to suit their needs for hundreds of years. Yeah, this is nothing new. Whoever has control espouses their definition so they can drive their adherents in their direction and their "adversaries" in the other. Paying attention to this is tantamount to running on a hamster wheel. When I look back at history, it is all the same. The people who achieve power make all the same mistakes as their "oppressors" did. Today, data and communication are power. In the Middle Ages they burned Bibles so people would not have access to data. In Germany they burned books to deprive people of data. In the 1960's they had racial and ethnic injustice in plain sight, but the media of that day kept the data hidden. I reference these years because it is unbelievable that people still did not get it, but it is a good example of my topic. Individuals have stood in the path of slavery, the Nazi's, civil rights abuses and more. It was the individuals that heard from God while their organizations sat by and watched. Today, the voice of the enemy and the world simply market their viewpoint in a manner that eliminates the view that is not agreeable. It did not work on citizens of The Kingdom historically, and it will not work on us today, but redefinition is a real tool of the demonic to make their view seem like truth, and there are many that consume the poison. Over the years many people and groups have attempted to claim that the Holocaust did not take place. I imagine, given enough time, this seed may take hold but, I hope not. Israel is a people chosen by the God of the Bible, my God, and they will always be persecuted (If you want to know more about this topic read Know My Voice I). If life as we know it continues to be redefined, like so many other important truths the world moves another step further from God.

Input vs Output

The game changer in the life of a human is when a person is willing to examine how and why they developed their perspective and are they willing to consider another perspective. To be able to see something thru the eyes of another is an important discipline. To embrace the other perspective is to embrace your own fears. I am not referring simply to the single view or ideology, because the daily challenge of change involves both. For example, if you are Hindu and come to the United States to live, you will encounter a culture that could make you fearful of losing your culture or religion It could make you fear that your children will embrace the American culture and minimize their own. The same is true if you are a Christian and move to Saudi Arabia or if you are a Jew and move to Iran. How about Muslims in China? Imagine a conservative embracing liberal ideals or vice versa. Oh, what a nightmare! This voice also speaks in another way. When individuals in a particular culture see another culture growing alongside them, the voice of fear speaks thoughts that make them afraid of change. This happened with every immigrant culture that emigrated to the United States. The Irish, Italians, Germans, Asians, Middle Eastern, African, etc. It is why slavery existed since the beginning of time. All cultures, races, ethnicities, and religions have been targeted at one time or another. This common fear is caused by the demonic voice, and it gives rise to hate and violence. Why is this important? Because the issues that plague mankind today are the same issues that plagued mankind for millennia[5]. We all know this! But we are just too broken to change, to stop listening to the wrong voices. Jesus lost it all because He refused to embrace the mob because they represent the voice of the demonic, the voice of hate, anger, and manipulation. And the mob mentality is on both sides[6]. Jesus stopped his own disciple from protecting him because he had to go to the cross. Peter thought violence was the answer. In the United States, we have cultural implications that want us to embrace the fear we will lose what we have gained. Asian, Latino, Jew, Black, White, Liberal,

---

[5] **Acts 6:1** In those days when the number of disciples was increasing, the Hellenistic Jews among them complained against the Hebraic Jews because their widows were being overlooked in the daily distribution of food.

[6] Simon Peter therefore having a sword, drew it, and struck the high priest's slave, and cut off his right ear; ... [11] Jesus therefore said to Peter, "Put the sword into the sheath; the cup which the Father has given Me, shall I not drink it?" (Joh 18:10-11 NAS)

Conservative, and other groups being pressed daily to hate each other. Here is where the daily perspective comes in to focus. We need to be open every day to the voice of the Holy Spirit and to reject the rhetoric and the bias planted not by the voice of the Holy Spirit but by the other voices. Consider the fact that the voice you are hearing does not care about the outcome, it just cares about controlling you. I encourage you to go for it! Adopting one new perspective only allows for a one-time challenge. I was a Roman Catholic. I was born again and became an Evangelical. Unfortunately, the new organizational mindset contained the same errors, only the name changed. We have all done this in various ways, only to become all the things we were within the original organizational data stream. We repeat the output with no growth. The daily challenge is to consider the perspective that cause us not to hate, not to fear, not to criticize, not to demean, not to fight, not to manipulate and the like! Developing a relationship with the Spirit of God is the only way to change the volume of the voices that cause us to wall ourselves into a corner in fear. There is a better way. God can be trusted directly. We people have been given an opportunity to have a relationship with God and consider the input that comes directly from the Creator[7]. And let me be noticeably clear, this is for all people, no matter who you are! Given God's input, you will realize that your output can get better, unless of course, you are totally satisfied with your current output.

Love your neighbor as yourself

The mind is complex. The complexity surrounds the fact that the mind is not simply corporeal. It is beyond the physical. So, to challenge one's perspective daily involves the most disciplinary practices that the mind can manage[8]. It is a process by where one corrals all thoughts, using some, discarding some, and holding others until the proper time arrives to utilize them. Releasing thoughts can be one of the greatest events in the life of a person, or it can be one of the most damaging. These thoughts can put you in the history books as a great person or they can destroy yourself

---

[7] 13 "But when He, the Spirit of truth, comes, He will guide you into all the truth; (Joh 16:13 NAS)

[8] We demolish arguments and every pretension that sets itself up against the knowledge of God, and we take captive every thought to make it obedient to Messiah. (2Cor 10:5)

and other people. Treating people as you want to be treated is the hallmark of this discipline, espoused in both the Bible and the Quran[9][10]. This discipline should be sought fervently and with hope. Hope that at the end of the day, you can validate yourself without guile and when you stand before the throne of the King, you will be exonerated by the sacrifice Jesus made for our brokenness. Keeping this practice, the task of loving one's neighbor becomes clearer ......but not necessarily easier, at first. True love is not a fleetingly static event. It is a growing dynamic process so, loving another is accomplished by comment and action. It is about your ability to feel what your neighbor feels. If accomplished, this feeling increases over time and the increase can be captured moment by moment. Verifiability and validation are obvious because you have a witness[11], the Spirit of God. This witness allows you to know and feel that what you are doing is worth it. Loving one's neighbor needs to be an inward and outward

---

[9] O you who believe! Be steadfast for God, bearing witness to justice and let not hatred for a people lead you to be unjust. Be Just: that is near to reverence. And reverence God. Surely God is aware of whatsoever you do. To those who believe and perform righteous deeds, God has promised forgiveness and great reward: Quran, The Table spread/al-Maidah 5:8-9

[10] 'You shall not take vengeance, nor bear any grudge against the sons of your people, but you shall love your neighbor as yourself; I am the LORD. (Lev 19:18 NAS)

[11] 16 But if I do judge, my decisions are true, because I am not alone. I stand with the Father, who sent me. John 8:16

experience. If not, it is empty behavior that ends in the doer knowing that their word was in vain and useless because it was not done in truth, it was not done selflessly, it was hypocritical. Pretending to mend a brokenness that can only be mended with God's truth is useless. The only way is relationship with God[12] by way of the Holy Spirit, the source of loving one's neighbor.

Iron Will

The great teacher Watchman Nee says that at our core we are "will", not body, not mind, not spirit, but will. Another teacher of our times, Disney, produced a movie called Iron Will. It was about a young man who, thru sheer will, wins a grueling dog sled race. The human will can be immensely powerful, it is probably all our power. Additionally, will was given to us free! Some of the most challenging times I have are to get people to change their mind, their direction, their will. My son and daughter-in-law said they had a most

---

[12] "And this is eternal life, that they may know You, the only true God, and Jesus the Messiah whom you have sent. (Joh 17:3 NAS)

challenging time to get their children to finish a tube of tooth paste before opening a new one. As a medical professional I have seen people, void of medical facts, follow the advice of a stranger they met in the aisle of the store over the advice of their own medical expert. The will of the human is the most difficult aspect to redirect once on a certain track. Human will power can be either positive or negative. When someone gets a bad medical diagnosis, it can debilitate them with fear, driven by the will. The will also can achieve the exact opposite. It can push someone through to experience victory in the most difficult and darkest times. Human will power is what moved Jesus to endure a horrible death when he was crucified. In Jesus' case, it also brought him to the cross, brought him to heal multitudes, brought him to be disciplined in listening to the voice of the Holy Spirit. Jesus utilized his will to direct his faith and action, he said it could move mountains. And in his case, it did! It brought us to where we are today. He is the single most influential person in history, all because of will. And his will moves multitudes today because the Holy Spirit affects the will of these people to change their lives, change that heals and guides and loves people from the inside, all because of Jesus. These are not necessarily Citizens who the Kingdom of God resides inside via relationship with the Holy Spirit, it could be anyone because God does not play favorites[13]. These people can be found in all religions, even atheists. The difference is the recognition of the source: The Holy Spirit. It is worth repeating; There was no historical figure that has had the impact that Jesus has had on humanity. He is alive, living within each of the Citizens of his Kingdom and reaching out to all people to draw them to the Father[14] so they can join the Kingdom, not some organization. There is an ongoing relationship, a voice, a conversation within each person. One does not have to "belong" to an organization. God speaks to all people in many ways. He uses all kinds of messengers. People, TV, movies, books, email, websites and more. His voice is a voice that can penetrate everything and that all have heard at one time or another, they just do not know it because religion has made God too hard to reach, to understand, to know. Are you willing to

---

[13] For there is no partiality with God. (Rom 2:11 NAS)

[14] 6 Jesus said to him, "I am the way, and the truth, and the life; no one comes to the Father, but through Me. (Joh 14:6 NAS)

change your mind? Your will? Listen, He is not far from you[15].

John the Immerser

The first question you have is, who is John the Immerser? We know this historical figure as John the Baptist. Here was an individual who heard the voice of God. John heard thru the social media of the day, which was family, culture, history, the scriptures Judaism and the Holy Spirit directly. He is a good example of a human focusing their will on God's will. We know that the people respected John. Even the secular Jewish/Roman historian Josephus had something to say about John[16] (and Jesus[17]). John had

---

[15] and He made from one, every nation of mankind to live on all the face of the earth, having determined *their* appointed times, and the boundaries of their habitation, [27] that they should seek God, if perhaps they might grope for Him and find Him, though He is not far from each one of us; [28] for in Him we live and move and exist, (Act 17:26-28 NAS)

[16] Now, some of the Jews thought that the destruction of Herod's army came from God, and that very justly, as a punishment for what he did against John, that was call the Baptist; For Herod slew him who was a good man and commanded the Jews to practice virtue both as to righteousness towards one another , and piety towards God......Josephus Antiq 18.5.2

[17] Now there was a man about this time Jesus, a wise man, if it be lawful to call him a man, for he was a doer of wonderful works – a teacher of such men as receive the truth with pleasure. He drew over to him both many of the Jews and many of the gentiles. He was the Messiah; (64) and when Pilate, at the suggestion of the principal men amongst us, had condemned him to the cross, those that loved him at the first did not forsake him, for he appeared to them alive again the third day, as the divine prophets had foretold these and ten thousand other wonderful things concerning him,; the tribe of Christians so named for him are not extinct at this day. Josephus Antiq 18.3.1ff

one job, to announce the Messiah. Society today wants people multi-tasking on the cell phone, computer, and texting, all at the same time. We have trouble focusing our will to hear God's voice and completing the task of listening to God because of all the distractions. Jesus validated John and his mission. Jesus said that no one born of a woman was greater than John because John preferred God's will over his own. He knew listening for the voice of the Holy Spirit was paramount. I know that it seems narrow to consider that a human being was born to do one job, but John's priority was God's will. People have similar priorities that engulf them. When a couple has a new child or a new pet, priorities change. They have one focus, to see to the needs of that new one in their life. People who own a business sometimes sacrifice everything to devote themselves solely to that business. John knew mankind was broken and he saw to needs, our needs. John had his priorities in the correct order. He fulfilled the task God gave him. John listened to the Holy Spirit, not the voice of the world[18]. He refused to be part of the organization of Judaism

---

[18] But when he saw many of the Pharisees and Sadducees coming for baptism, he said to them, "You brood of vipers, who warned you to flee from the wrath to come? (Mat 3:7 NAS)

and preferred to be a citizen of the Kingdom. Do you have a task from God?

Inception

Inception is defined as the genesis, the starting point for any activity. There is a movie by the same name, and it involved planting a thought into the mind of an individual without their knowledge as to its genesis. I strongly believe in the four voices speaking thoughts into our minds, so inception is important. These voices plant ideas or thoughts and we must identify the source to properly govern its affect. We govern them by lending our will for, or against such thoughts. Once we decide the source, will is in the driver's seat. One example is fear. In forty plus years of pharmacy practice I have seen many patients whose will is driving some fear that lives in their mind. It replicates itself using a host of potential disasters that may arrive at their front door. Their inability to understand this concept only adds to the problem. Another example is politics. The politicians via the media drives fear in the minds of people of all political views. And then there is religion. The rules and regulations of religious organizations can drive people to either cling to their organization senselessly or reject religion completely. The voice of self, the demonic, and the voice of the world speak to three of the four voices that affect our consciousness. All these plant thoughts into the mind of each and every one of us[19]. Recognizing the source is paramount.

The voice of God is much more subtle yet noteworthy. It is that thought whereby a curiosity flags in one's mind...... and that is the moment to seize, to not only consider the genesis of the thought but to recognize the voice of God! God's voice is different than the others. I have found that often, when God's voice speaks, I find myself saying; "where did that come from?" In many cases I have found it to be a self-challenging thought, a thought that would go against self-support. I find that it usually wants me to be selfless in some way. Once we ID the source, we can try to direct our will to work for God. Inception is crucial.

---

[19] But turning around and seeing His disciples, He rebuked Peter, and said, "Get behind Me, Satan; for you are not setting your mind on God's interests, but man's." (Mar 8:33 NAS)

The Passion

The Passion of Jesus of Nazareth, not the movie, the actual event, is the core of this book's message because out of that event came mankind's relationship with the Holy Spirit. Prior to this event God used specific individuals to speak for Him. The Passion is the event that fulfilled the words of the prophet Jeremiah[20]. The Kingdom of God intricately and foundationally stands on this event because it provides all the evidence that The Messiah was not building a tax exempt religious 501c3. According to the Bible there are only two classes of people. The class that is either serving God or the class that is serving sin[21]. It is exceedingly rare for me to use the word sin because it is a bias trigger that shuts one's mind down to conversation. But I need to use it here for a specific reason. Sin, as literally defined in the Bible, is when someone makes a bad decision. What is the premise of bad decisions? In our society, and world, this premise is dynamic and fluid. We make

---

[20] "But this is the covenant which I will make with the house of Israel after those days," declares the LORD, "I will put My law within them, and on their heart I will write it; and I will be their God, and they shall be My people. (Jer 31:33 NAS)

[21] Jesus answered them, "Truly, truly, I say to you, everyone who commits sin is the slave of sin. [35] "And the slave does not remain in the house forever; the son does remain forever. [36] "If therefore the Son shall make you free, you shall be free indeed. (Joh 8:34-36 NAS)

many decisions in just a day. Mankind has been making decisions for millennia. Poor decision making is the reason we fight wars and hate one another. When one group feels oppressed or discriminated against by another, we have disagreement. Both sides see their argument as valid and right. Human rights violators who execute gays for being gay is just one example of poor decision making. Let me explain.

The Bible presents a dichotomy concerning certain topics. In Micah it calls for mercy, compassion, and justice. In Exodus it calls for the stoning of men who have sex with men. Which is correct? When Jesus gave his life for the people, wasn't it for all the people? He exchanged his life for our bad attitudes, for our bad decisions, our brokenness, for our incorrect judgments. And Jesus' exchange was meant to help us break free from bad decision making. Lack of compassion toward another person is a bad decision in God's opinion. As mentioned earlier, to change one's mind is only possible for the mind's owner. No one can change someone else's mind. So as an example, Jesus changed his mind and became the object that received the justice that was required by The Father for all bad decision making. It was his passion to fix us by breaking himself. It may sound weird but, how many times have you put yourself between you and someone else to prevent them from getting hurt in some manner? It takes passion!

To The Leadership

My good friend Bill (a true leader in the Kingdom) has had a way of producing some of the most profound conclusions concerning some of life's most common occurrences. Did you ever think about the reality of reserved parking spaces or reserved seating? A couple of years ago, Paul McCartney and Ringo Star reunited in a Beatles special. I did not watch the entire performance but, the little that I did see, I noticed Tom Hanks and his wife in the front row center of the audience. It could have been some poor homeless person but, these types of privileges are not reserved for those people. A few years back we were renting a space for our Friday night worship service from another congregation. The sanctuary was arranged with chairs, as opposed to pews. In the front row, two chairs were separated from the rest of the row by a small table. One of the individuals on the worship team innocently asked, who sits in those two seats? My friend Bill quickly replied, "someone who thinks they are important", profound! In the book of the Bible written by James, he is noticeably clear about what our attitude as leaders should be. He is also noticeably clear that we will be accountable for that attitude[22].

Relationship, connection, dependency

Human life demonstrates that when a baby is born there exists the reality of dependency. Relationship with others is similar. It is vitally important, but it cannot happen successfully because it is fundamentally dependent on something else. When one entity has a dependency on another entity, it implies that the one entity cannot function alone. God is the source of everything. Everything is dependent on God, including relationship. Relationship is defined as having some type of connection with someone or something else. In a car the drive shaft is connected to

---

[22] Let not many *of you* become teachers, my brethren, knowing that as such we shall incur a stricter judgment. (Jam 3:1 NAS)

the engine, they have relationship. In this case the drive shaft is dependent on the engine to turn it so the car can move.

In the case of humanity, humans, physically, have no need of connection with each other. The movie Castaway is a good example. The character survived without any other humans being present, he needed no connection there. But human to human connection seems important. In the case of Castaway, that same character developed relationship with a soccer ball, an imaginary companion, a substitute. God determined the value of relationship back in the Garden of Eden[23]. The term relate is defined as showing sympathy for, or identifying with, another. Relating is functional exercise. I want to expose a fallacy concerning human relationship. Stated simply, when two humans engage in disagreement, argument, and the like, I contend this is not relationship. I also contend we must stop this behavior. The effects of disfunction between people all produce negative results of varying degrees. This disfunction masquerades as relationship. Disfunction is the definition of relationships that have gone awry.

---

[23] Then the LORD God said, "It is not good for the man to be alone; I will make him a helper suitable for him." (Gen 2:18 NAS)

When a family is labeled dysfunctional, our psychologists attempt to find the reasons and source behind the actions and attitudes of the individuals. Because humanity is broken, we have created a dependence on disfunction, this is interaction with the lack of relationship. There is no connection between the individuals, only collision. The engine may be running but, it is not turning the drive shaft. The car is not moving, the metal is grinding, shards are being shot all over, the car is stagnant, crippled and useless for its intended purpose, and so it is with broken human dysfunction labeled as relationship.

For decades television and movies have provided happy endings and lessons learned. It may have been useful; I am not quite sure. Today, television producers have become so bold that they create reality shows which embrace anger, frustration, and hate, portraying disfunction as the new standard. Ratings soar and I am saddened. The voices of the demonic, the world and self are drowning out the voice of God. Why do we want to see people fighting, yelling, crying and pushed to brink of violence? We were created for more. On the other end of the spectrum, the few shows and movies that demonstrate functional relationship cause us to ask the question, why can't my life be like this? But still, it is only pretend. Our failures at relationship have society taking antidepressants, anxiolytics, sedatives and more. We KNOW there can be more, we just don't understand that relationship is a functional connection, but in humanity's case all that remains is to embrace disfunction as the connection.

It is not normal for people to hate other people just because they disagree. Disruption is not relationship, compassion[24] is relationship!

So, if relationship requires functional connection that creates a dependency, this dependency requires people to work at the positive, useful, and inclusive nature of this connection. Consider this; hating another human, any human being, may disqualify one from actually being able to love. Even though Judas betrayed Jesus, it is never recorded that Jesus hated him. In fact, Judas, being a sinner, was one of the many sinners that Jesus died for on the cross. Did you ever ask yourself if it is possible that both love and hate can

---

[24] "But I say to you, love your enemies, and pray for those who persecute you [45] in order that you may be sons of your Father who is in heaven; for He causes His sun to rise on *the* evil and *the* good, and sends rain on *the* righteous and *the* unrighteous. (Mat 5:44-45 NAS)

(or should) exist in you, or come out of you[25]? A long time ago, I heard someone say, "we judge others on their results, but we judge ourselves on our intention." This is an enormously powerful thought. It is dependent on you to work toward connection, toward relationship. And that includes all connections. They must be rational, compassionate, and merciful. This is how God functions. Not because these attributes are separate from God, but because they emanate from God. We must be singular in our understanding. God does not hate humans. God hates evil activity or actions, but God has nothing but compassion for humanity[26]. So, when we see other humans' actions focused on disconnections, we must understand that hating the person is not the answer. It will not resolve anything. But connection can and will present the opportunity to relate. And that relationship is dependent on THE CONNECTION, Jesus! Jesus is the source of connection. He has sent the Holy Spirit to connect humans to God. When that connection is

---

[25] Does a fountain send out from the same opening *both* fresh and bitter *water*? [12] Can a fig tree, my brethren, produce olives, or a vine produce figs? Neither *can* salt water produce fresh. (Jam 3:11-12 NAS)

[26] "For God so loved the world, that He gave His only begotten Son, that whoever believes in Him should not perish, but have eternal life. (Joh 3:16 NAS)

functioning, we can develop relationship human to human. We cannot have the horizontal, human to human relationship, if the vertical, human to God, relationship does not exist. Without God, relationship is moot. Without God, relationship is smoke and mirrors. Without God, there is no connection to the engine. The car is not going anywhere.

The current state of affairs

The current state of affairs is anger! Everyone is angry and it is mostly attributed to human brokenness, but humans can change. I understand that we don't like to think of people as angry, especially ourselves, but it is true. I have worked for years to quell the demonic disruptive voice that ushers me toward anger. The car in front of yours is going too slow. The car that just passed yours is going too fast. The person in the grocery store is blocking the aisle with their carriage. The checkout line is too long. All the parking spaces close to the store are taken. I have spent hours and hours on the computer and cannot get an appointment for my Covid shot. I could go on and on. I was there! But the voice of the Holy Spirit silenced those other voices. Would you like them silenced? It takes an attitude change. Jesus attempted to achieve this with the parable of the good Samaritan[27]. He asked, who is your neighbor? I have high school classmates that navel gaze constantly on politics. They are "smart" about it. They don't come off angry, but they are very angry. It does not matter what side of the fence you are on. All that matters is that you are on a side. Walking the fence line is not easy, but that is where God is to be found. Being on a side is how the demonic forces keep you hooked into anger. We need to break free. It really does not matter what I think politically, socially, economically, spiritually, or financially, what matters is that I can love others, even someone who hates me. Let me offer a silly exercise in taking control of your thoughts. I have been driving for some forty-five years. Many of those years included the exchange of a glance as I made a left in front of another vehicle, or another vehicle made a left in front of mine. It was not

---

[27] "But a certain Samaritan, who was on a journey, came upon him; and when he saw him, he felt compassion, [34] and came to him, and bandaged up his wounds, pouring oil and wine on *them*; and he put him on his own beast, and brought him to an inn, and took care of him. (Luk 10:33-34 NAS)

necessarily an angry glare all the time. Sometimes it was simply an "I am in a hurry, and I wish you were not on the road at this moment" look. Sometimes it was a smile and hello but, this is a rare occurrence. You know what I am referring to because we all have experienced the event. I can offer more scenarios, but I am sure you can think of some yourself. My point is that most of the times when this occurs, you trade an eye-to-eye exchange. Many of us, at those moments, wonder what we did wrong or worse, accuse another with our look. So, here is my solution. When I turn by another vehicle, I never make eye contact. Yes, I am the guy you look at and say, "what planet is this fellow on?" But it does not make the other person wonder why I was staring at them. It does not feed the beast. At the same time, I am very careful about vehicle safety. There are many ways the Holy Spirit can quiet the voices of the enemy. One simply needs to embrace the voice of peace, goodness, gentleness, and patience. We need to work with God to love one another. Historically, mankind has hated mankind for millennia and for no good reason. There is, on the other hand a great reason to love. The other person really needs it!

A god Made by Man

The Bible is noticeably clear that there are many gods. Mankind has been worshipping them for millennia in the form of nature, animals, humans, rocks and more. In the three main religions attached to the bible, Judaism, Christianity and Islam, each has their main spiritual being. Judaism has Elohim, Yahweh, Adonai or G-D. Christianity has The Father, The Son and The Holy Spirit. Islam has Allah. Within these three religions exist quite a few sects or denominations. What had occurred to me years ago is that the groups within the same religion don't necessarily worship the same god. What I mean to say is, for example, different Christian denominations worship different Jesus's. You may ask, how is that possible? There is only one Jesus. Ah, but is there? For example, there is a particular church has protests at the funerals of fallen military personnel because they think war is wrong, so they act with a lack of compassion toward other humans who are hurting due to loss. This offers the impression that the god they worship also lacks compassion. This is not the God of the Bible[28], this is another god, another Jesus, an imposter. Another example concerns the Jehovah's Witness Organization and Evangelical Christians. The evangelicals believe Jesus is not created but he and The Father are One God, it is a unique relationship that is unexplainable. The Jehovah's Witnesses believe Jesus is a creation of Jehovah. Two different Jesus's by the groups using virtually the same Bible! My conclusion in this matter was made on the fact that the behavior of each of the groups could not be predicated on the same historical data and the figure Jesus. Their understanding of Jesus caused doctrines that were diametrically opposed to one another so, it could not possibly be the same person. This is true also for Jews. Chasidim, Reconstructionist, Reform, and Orthodox all behave so different that their God cannot be the same for all of them. This is true also for the Muslim community. Shia and Sunni behave and believe differently.

So, I must conclude that God is not necessarily who He says He is, <u>he is who we say he is</u>! The bible agrees

---

[28] And when He went ashore, He saw a great multitude, and He felt compassion for them because they were like sheep without a shepherd; and He began to teach them many things. (Mar 6:34 NAS)

with me and in the case of Jesus, there are those whom He will disown[29] because of this snafus. So, too often god is made by mankind. We make him who we want him to be. This leads to the creation of a fault ridden god. A being that can be manipulated at a debate between atheist and minister to be weak, indecisive, and defective. Religious organizations rarely give God the chance to be God so, doctrine, ritual and organization become god.

Citizens of the Kingdom cannot be afraid to let God be God to accomplish His purpose, after all, He has been doing this quite a while now. We must trust God beyond our understanding. We must let God guide us and help us to change. God wants compassionate forgiving worshipers. God want those who submit to Him to demonstrate it with their actions driven from a spirit connected to The Spirit of God. God wants a relationship whereby we understand that He created us to be His people and that we should be different because He is different[30]. God does not want a people

---

[29] "Many will say to Me on that day, 'Lord, Lord, did we not prophesy in Your name, and in Your name cast out demons, and in Your name perform many miracles?' [23] "And then I will declare to them, 'I never knew you; depart from Me, you who practice lawlessness.' (Mat 7:22-23 NAS)

[30] 'For I am the LORD your God. Consecrate yourselves therefore, and be holy; for I am holy. (Lev 11:44 NAS)

who reduce Him to a puppet that changes with their every changing emotion. I encourage you to let God find you, so you can find Him. I encourage you to press God for an encounter. I encourage you not to make a god in your image because that god will never be great enough to help you, because he can never be greater than you. If you strive after <u>the One true God</u>, I promise you will learn firsthand that He will never be anything other than What He Will Be, God.

The Kingdom of God

I have written much about each person being able to hear from the Holy Spirit directly. This is true for all people. Listening to, as compared to obeying, the voice is a bit more challenging. When Jesus ascended, he sent the Holy Spirit to be a companion for all who embrace him as Messiah. The Holy Spirit is a deposit in the spiritual bank of God[31]. Therefore, Messiah is unique and necessary. This deposit makes all the

---

[31] 13 In Him, you also, after listening to the message of truth, the gospel of your salvation-- having also believed, you were sealed in Him with the Holy Spirit of promise, (Eph 1:13 NAS)

difference for your future. I ask you a very serious question. Does life matter to you? While you ponder that question, I ask another question. How do you determine what really matters to you? It is a serious question that requires some serious thought. In our current world, I don't see The Kingdom of God being important to people, and I know why. Organizations have made God irrelevant.

To some, let's call them group A, God is a non-starter. I applaud you for your honesty and I will get back to you in a little bit. Then there is group B. This group shows up on a holy day to either invoke some sense of connection with God or with other people. Who the connection is with is not important, in the end it is just for show and even the hypocrites know they are hypocrites. Then we have group C. This group participates much more in religious life. They seem to be players. I believe it is because they have some desire within to want God. The problem is they usually get involved in a system (organization) that appears to have a real connection to God, but simply occupies their time with liturgical processes that partially fulfills their desire. They are always looking for God everywhere but within. Then there is group D. These individuals are the most deceived, and it includes many "leaders". They see the organization as their validation. They usually hold various types of office or have some sort of title. They are exalted by people. They will tell you they do not want to be honored while they are enjoying the benefits.

The Kingdom of God is within you[32] is the message of the Messiah. I am disheartened that many people I know keep looking for the Kingdom out in the world. I applaud group A because while they are the most distant, they are the most vulnerable. Historically, some of the most on fire people of God had some of the hardest hearts[33]. The bigger they are, the harder they fall. I know this from experience.

To all, the Kingdom of God is not far from you. It is not hard to become a part of it and you don't need to join any earthly organization. If you sincerely seek Messiah Jesus, He will meet with you and walk with you on a journey that was designed explicitly for you. Any challenges you find will be offset by the benefits you experience. The road has some hills and some

---

[32] for the kingdom of God is not eating and drinking, but righteousness and peace and joy in the Holy Spirit. (Rom 14:17 NAS)

[33] "And when we had all fallen to the ground, I heard a voice saying to me in the Hebrew dialect, 'Saul, Saul, why are you persecuting Me? It is hard for you to kick against the goads.' (Act 26:14 NAS)

valleys. You will learn the most in the valleys and you will come to appreciate those experiences more than the level or high ground. Why? Because the valleys teach us how to act when we are on the mountain top. This is indispensable. It is what we are judged on. The Kingdom is the presence of the Holy Spirit living within you. You can be a citizen of the greatest Kingdom in creation, you simply need to show up every day. God does!

John's other Books